WHERE ON EARTH?
MAPPING PARTS OF THE WORLD

THE EQUATOR

EQUATOR

By Todd Bluthenthal

Gareth Stevens
PUBLISHING

ECUADOR 0°-0°LAT.

Please visit our website, www.garethstevens.com. For a free color catalog of all our high-quality books, call toll free 1-800-542-2595 or fax 1-877-542-2596.

Cataloging-in-Publication Data
Names: Bluthenthal, Todd.
Title: The equator / Todd Bluthenthal.
Description: New York : Gareth Stevens Publishing, 2018. | Series: Where on Earth? mapping parts of the world | Includes index.
Identifiers: ISBN 9781482464214 (pbk.) | ISBN 9781482464238 (library bound) | ISBN 9781482464221 (6 pack)
Subjects: LCSH: Latitude–Juvenile literature. | Geographical positions–Juvenile literature.
Classification: LCC QB224.5 B58 2017 | DDC 526'.6–dc23

Published in 2018 by
Gareth Stevens Publishing
111 East 14th Street, Suite 349
New York, NY 10003

Designer: Samantha DeMartin
Editor: Joan Stoltman

Photo credits: series art CHAPLIA YAROSLAV/Shutterstock.com; cover, pp. 1 (map), 9 Intrepix/Shutterstock.com; cover, p. 1 (inset) Fotos593/Shutterstock.com; p. 5 Ibrahim Burganov/Shutterstock.com; p. 7 Istimages/Shutterstock.com; p. 11 Bardocz Peter/Shutterstock.com; p. 13 Vitoriano Junior/Shutterstock.com; p. 15 Aphelleon/Shutterstock.com; p. 17 sebikus/Shutterstock.com; p. 19 edeantoine/Shutterstock.com; p. 21 (inset) Cristina Simon/Shutterstock.com; p. 21 (main) frees/Shutterstock.com.

Printed in the United States of America

CPSIA compliance information: Batch #CS17GS: For further information contact Gareth Stevens, New York, New York at 1-800-542-2595.

CONTENTS

Boldface words appear in the glossary.

What Is the Equator?

The equator is an imaginary line on maps. It runs around Earth like a belt, cutting Earth into two halves. These halves are called the Northern and Southern **Hemispheres**. The equator is one of many **parallel** lines of **latitude** that circle Earth.

equator

Latitude is measured in **degrees**, which is shown by the sign °. The equator is 0° latitude. All other lines of latitude measure distance from the equator. The farthest points from the equator are the North and South Poles. They are found at 90° latitude.

90° south latitude

Water and Land

The equator is the longest line of latitude—almost 25,000 miles (40,200 km) long! It mostly passes through water, including the Pacific Ocean, the Atlantic Ocean, and the Indian Ocean. The land it goes through includes parts of Africa and South America.

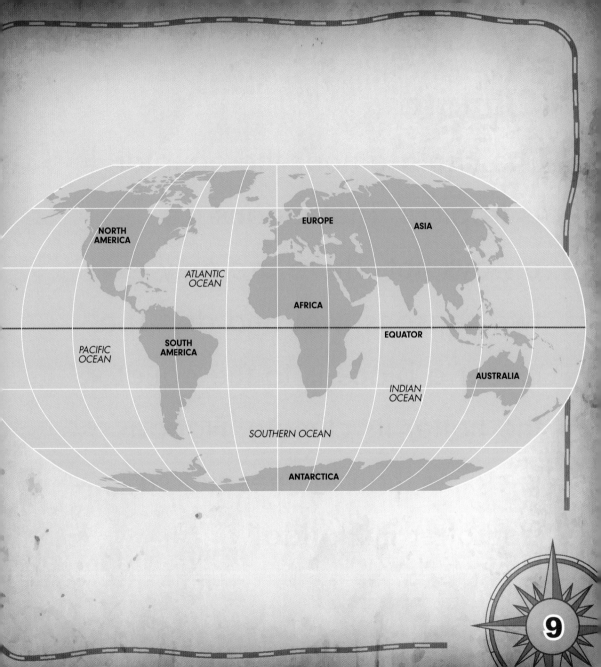

NORTH
AMERICA

EUROPE

ASIA

ATLANTIC
OCEAN

AFRICA

EQUATOR

PACIFIC
OCEAN

SOUTH
AMERICA

AUSTRALIA

INDIAN
OCEAN

SOUTHERN OCEAN

ANTARCTICA

Climate

The **climate** near the equator is tropical. That means it's always hot. There are only two seasons: wet and dry! The closer a place is to the equator, the hotter its climate. Florida is closer than Minnesota, so it's hotter in Florida!

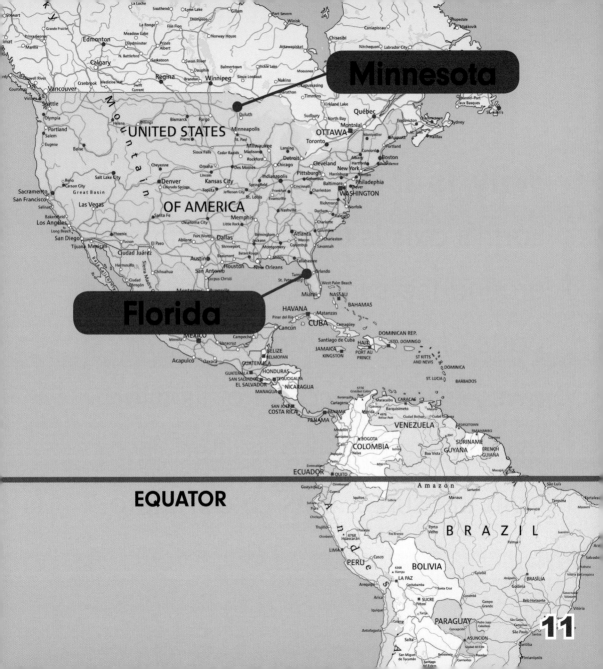

Minnesota

Florida

EQUATOR

Why Is It So Hot?

Earth's **axis** is **tilted**. As Earth moves around the sun throughout the year, parts of it tip toward the sun or away from it because of its tilted axis. When an area is tilted away from the sun, it gets colder there.

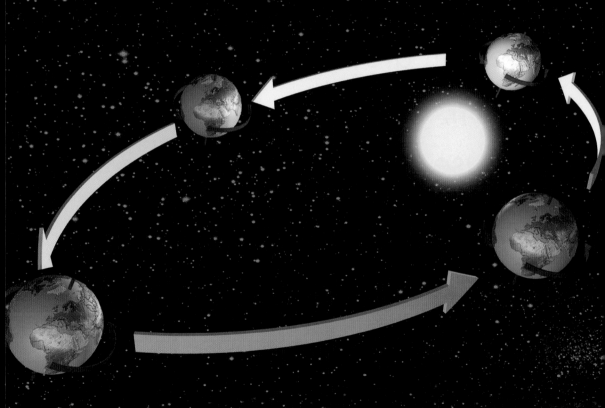

When an area is tilted toward the sun, it gets warmer there. Because the equator runs right around the middle of Earth, it's always tilted toward the sun. This means it's always hot there!

sun

sun's rays

Earth

Day and Night

Earth is spinning, or rotating, all the time. Each spin takes 24 hours, or 1 day, to finish. When an area on Earth faces the sun, it's daytime there. When it turns away from the sun, it's nighttime there.

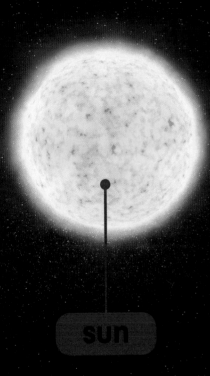

daytime on Earth

sun

nighttime on Earth

In most places on Earth, daytime and nighttime lengths change with the seasons throughout the year. But this doesn't happen at places near the equator. Near the equator, daytime and nighttime are always about 12 hours long each!

rainforest near the equator

19

Snow at the Equator?

Some places near the equator aren't tropical, though! As you get higher in the mountains of South America and Africa, it gets cooler. Cayambe, a **volcano** in South America, is the highest point on the equator. It has snow!

VENEZUELA

GUYANA

FRENCH
GUIANA

SURINAME

COLOMBIA

EQUATOR

CAYAMBE

ECUADOR

SOUTH AMERICA

PERU

BRAZIL

BOLIVIA

PARAGUAY

ATLANTIC
OCEAN

PACIFIC
OCEAN

CHILE

URUGUAY

ARGENTINA

snowy Cayambe

GLOSSARY

axis: an imaginary straight line around which a planet turns

climate: the common weather of a place over a period of time

degrees: the unit of measurement for latitude

hemisphere: one-half of Earth

latitude: one of the imaginary lines on maps that run east and west above and below the equator

parallel: telling about lines that are equally far apart at all points

tilted: not exactly up and down

volcano: an opening in a planet's surface through which hot, liquid rock sometimes flows

FOR MORE INFORMATION

BOOKS

Olien, Rebecca. *Longitude and Latitude*. New York, NY: Children's Press, 2013.

Parker, Victoria. *How Far Is Far? Comparing Geographical Distances*. Chicago, IL: Heinemann Library, 2011.

Waldron, Melanie. *Mapping the World*. Chicago, IL: Capstone Raintree, 2012.

WEBSITES

Around the World
timeforkids.com/around-the-world
Travel around the world—through your computer!

Day and Night
theschoolrun.com/homework-help/day-and-night
Read all about how day, night, and seasons work!

INDEX